Country ABCs

China
ABCs

A Book About the People
and Places of China

Written by Holly Schroeder   •   Illustrated by Jeff Yesh

Special thanks to our advisers for their expertise:
Joseph R. Allen, Ph.D.
Professor of Chinese Literature
University of Minnesota, Twin Cities

Susan Kesselring, M.A., Literacy Educator
Rosemount-Apple Valley-Eagan (Minnesota) School District

PICTURE WINDOW BOOKS
Minneapolis, Minnesota

Managing Editor: Bob Temple
Creative Director: Terri Foley
Editor: Nadia Higgins
Editorial Adviser: Andrea Cascardi
Copy Editor: Laurie Kahn
Designer: John Moldstad
Page production: Picture Window Books
The illustrations in this book were prepared digitally.

Picture Window Books
1710 Roe Crest Drive
North Mankato, MN 56003
www.capstonepub.com

Library of Congress Cataloging-in-Publication Data
Schroeder, Holly.
China ABCs : a book about the people and places of China /
Written by Holly Schroeder ; illustrated by Jeff Yesh.
p. cm. — (Country ABCs)
Summary: An alphabetical exploration of the people, geography, animals, plants,
history, and culture of China. Includes bibliographical references and index.
ISBN 978-1-4048-0180-6 (hardcover)
ISBN 978-1-4048-0358-9 (paperback)
1. China—Juvenile literature. 2. English language—
Alphabet—Juvenile literature. [1. China. 2. Alphabet.]
I. Yesh, Jeff, 1971- ill. II. Title. III. Series.
DS706 .S36 2004
951—dc22
2003016514

Printed in the United States   4674

Ni hao! (nee how)

That's how people say "hello!" in China. China is a huge country in eastern Asia. More than one billion people live there—about one-fifth of all the people in the world. More people live in China than in any other country.

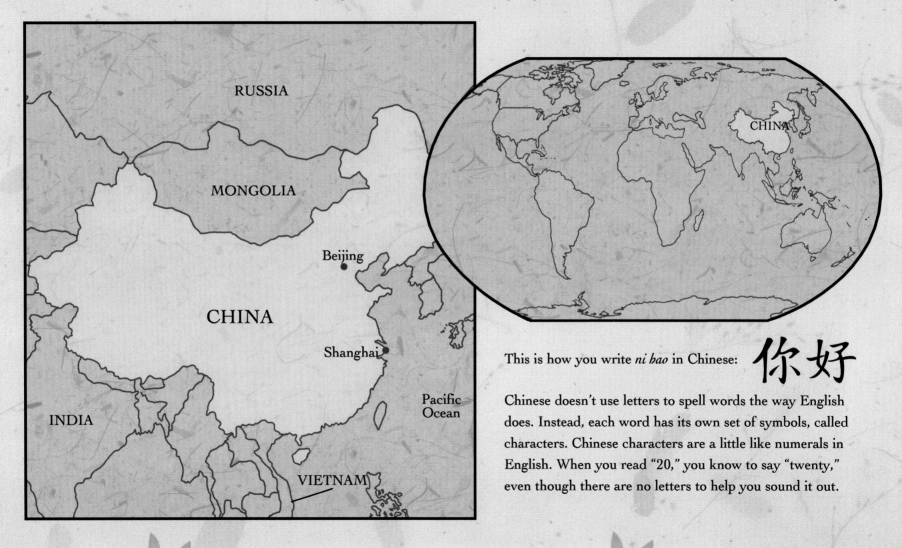

This is how you write *ni hao* in Chinese: 你好

Chinese doesn't use letters to spell words the way English does. Instead, each word has its own set of symbols, called characters. Chinese characters are a little like numerals in English. When you read "20," you know to say "twenty," even though there are no letters to help you sound it out.

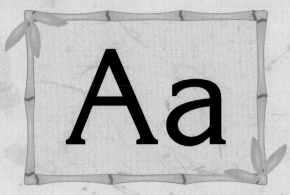

Aa

A is for *acupuncture*.

Acupuncture is an ancient Chinese way of treating illness. Doctors stick long, thin needles into special spots on a person's skin. The needles pinch a little at first, but they don't harm the skin.

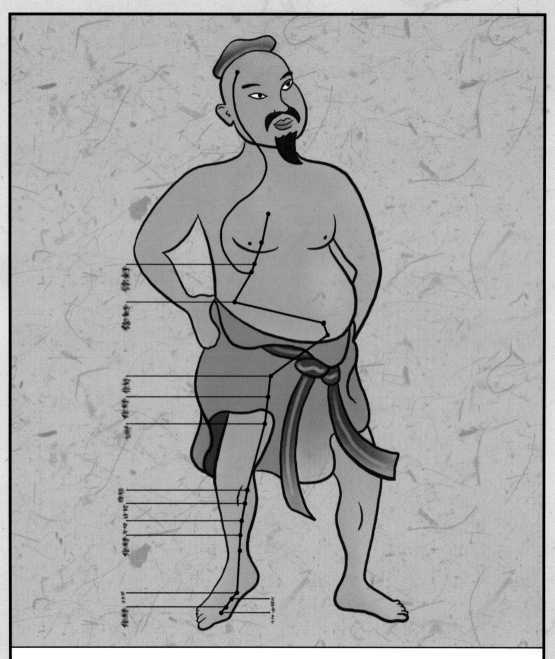

This picture is similar to a Chinese medical drawing from hundreds of years ago.

Bb

Very few people in China can afford to buy a car. Many people get around by riding bicycles. They put their belongings in a basket and pedal where they need to go.

FAST FACT: People also scoot around on motorcycles or hitch a ride on buses. For travel between cities, people often take the train.

B is for bicycles.

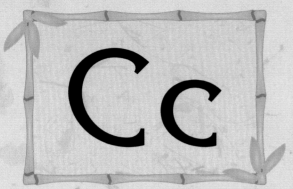

Cc

The calligraphy on this page is of the character *fu*, which means "good luck."

Calligraphy is the ancient art of writing with a brush dipped in ink. Many people in China hang poems or sayings written in beautiful calligraphy on their walls.

FAST FACT: Some Chinese characters have as many as 26 lines, which must be made in the correct order.

6

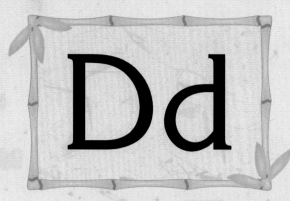

Dd

D is for dragon.

The Chinese dragon does not breathe fire. In China, this beast is a symbol of good luck. The colorful creature is said to bring money and fame. It also brings rain for farmers.

FAST FACT: *People decorate rowboats to look like dragons for the yearly Dragon Boat Festival.*

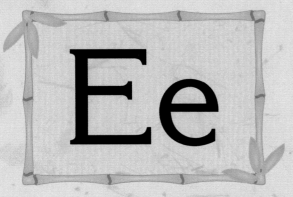

E is for Everest.

In Tibet, along China's southern edge, rises the highest mountain in the world—Mount Everest. Its icy peak stands 5½ miles (almost 9 kilometers) above sea level. Many people have died trying to climb the mountain. Sir Edmund Hillary and Tenzing Norgay were the first people to reach the top, in 1953.

FAST FACT: *Along with mountains, China's landscape includes hot deserts, treeless plains, and green meadows. About half of China's land is too hot or too cold for many people to live on.*

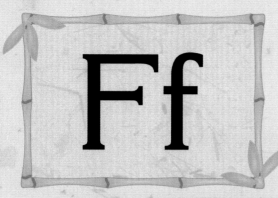

Ff

F is for flag.

The large yellow star of China's flag stands for the government. The four small stars around it represent China's people. The red color symbolizes the revolution of 1949, which created China's present-day government.

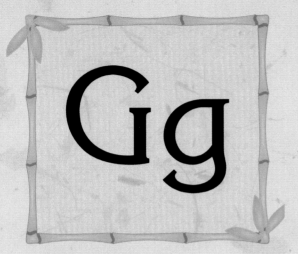

G is for Great Wall.

The Great Wall is China's most famous landmark. At 4,500 miles (7,240 kilometers), it is the longest structure ever built. Ancient Chinese rulers forced millions of ordinary people to build the wall. The work was done completely by hand.

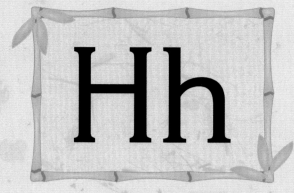

Hh

China is the place for hats. In rice fields, farmers wear huge bamboo hats to shade their eyes from the sun. In cold areas, hats are trimmed with fur. Merchants in cities wear simple cotton caps. During celebrations, people in traditional costumes parade down the street wearing tall headdresses that sparkle in the sun.

Ii

I is for incense.

When heated, incense powder makes a sweet-smelling smoke. Buddhists burn incense during religious ceremonies. Buddhism is one of China's main religions. Chinese Buddhists believe in life after death. They pray to many gods for help in times of trouble.

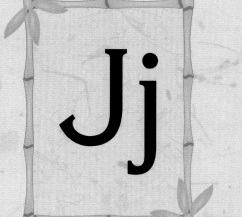

J is for jade.

In China, jade is called the stone of heaven. Jade is a hard, shiny stone that comes in purple, pink, yellow, green, and white. Many Chinese people believe jade has special powers to bring good health and keep evil spirits away. Parents often give their children jade gifts as wedding presents.

FAST FACT: *In the 1700s, China was ruled by an emperor who liked very detailed jade statues. During this time, an artist might have spent his whole life working on a single piece.*

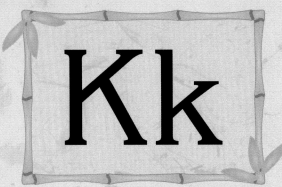

Kk

K is for kites.

Chinese people invented kites more than 2,000 years ago. The first kites were made of silk and bamboo. People wrote messages on the kites and sent them into the sky. They hoped their messages would be received by heavenly spirits. Today, flying kites is a popular pastime in China.

FAST FACT: Besides kites, the Chinese invented paper and printing, silk, fireworks, wheelbarrows, and compasses.

L is for lotus root.

Lotus root is crunchy like a carrot but tastes like fresh coconut. It is one of the many kinds of vegetables eaten in China. Chinese people eat vegetables with rice or noodles. They drink tea at every meal and use chopsticks instead of forks.

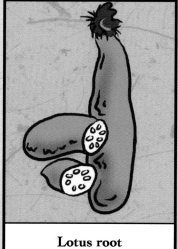

Lotus root

FAST FACT: Chinese food is usually stir-fried. Thin slices of meat and vegetables are cooked very quickly in a big, curved pan called a wok.

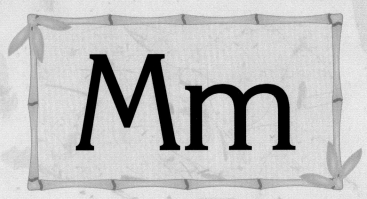

Mm

M is for Mao Zedong.

Fifty years ago, Mao Zedong was one of the most powerful people in the world. He was China's first communist leader. In a communist country, the government owns almost everything. Today, the leader of the Communist Party is still the most powerful person in China's government. But China's communist government is changing. It is allowing more and more people to open their own businesses.

Nn

N is for New Year.

Chinese New Year is an important family holiday, much in the same way that Thanksgiving is in the United States and Canada. People travel long distances to spend New Year's Day with their families. They pour into the streets to watch parades and light firecrackers. They carry huge paper dragons through the crowded streets.

FAST FACT: New Year in China depends on the moon calendar. It usually starts at the end of January.

O is for opera.

Chinese children love to go to the opera, where performers in colorful robes and painted faces act out familiar stories. Chinese opera stars don't just sing. They dance, mime, and do acrobatics, too.

FAST FACT: *Long ago, Chinese operas were performed in the street. The performers banged on gongs and drums to get the outdoor crowds to notice them. Today, operas in theaters still begin with this loud clanging of instruments.*

P is for Ping-Pong.

Pp

Ping pang qiu (ping pang chew) is the Chinese word for Ping-Pong, or table tennis. It is one of China's national sports. Ping-Pong players look like dancers as they bob and hop to hit the whizzing ball.

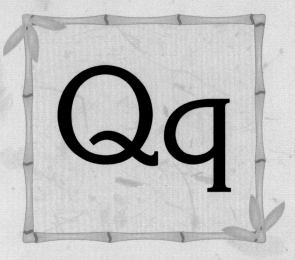

Q is for Qing (cheng) Dynasty.

For thousands of years, China was ruled by emperors. When one emperor died, his son or another male relative would take over. A dynasty is a period of time when all the emperors came from the same family. The Qing Dynasty was China's last dynasty. It lasted from 1644 to 1911.

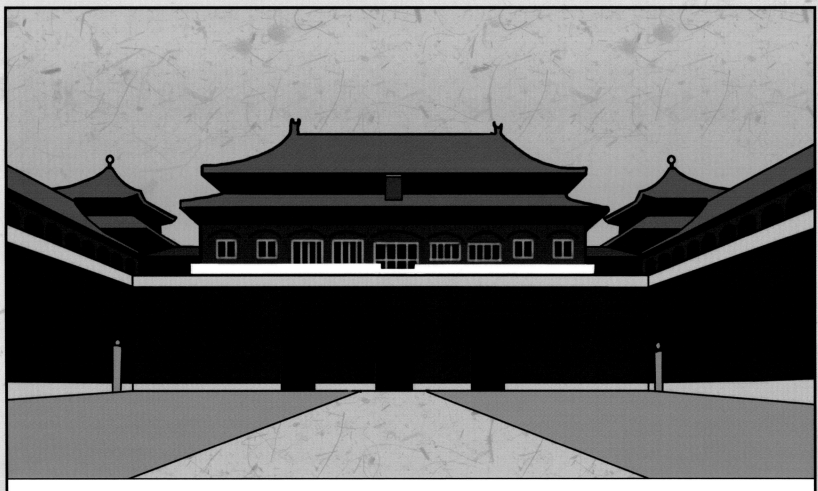

This palace is from a group of magnificent palaces called the Forbidden City. This is where Qing emperors lived.

Rr

R is for rice.

China is the world's biggest producer of rice. Rice is grown in watery fields called rice paddies, just as it was in ancient times. Most food in southern China is served with rice, and parents encourage children to eat every grain. They believe it is bad luck to leave a bowl spotted with rice grains.

FAST FACT: *China grows more cotton and wheat than any other country, too. It is also the world's largest producer of coal.*

Ss

S is for Shanghai (shang–HI).

This crowded, fast-paced city is China's largest, with more than 12 million people. The word *shanghai* means "upon the sea." Shanghai has served as China's major trading port for many years. Today, it is a leading center of Chinese industry and banking.

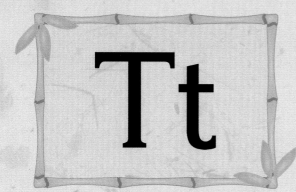

Tt

T is for Tiananmen
(TYEN-an-men) Square.

In 1989, thousands of students gathered at Tiananmen Square in China's capital city, Beijing. They wanted more freedom from China's communist government. The students knew they were putting themselves in danger by speaking out. Many of them died when the Chinese army used force to end the protest.

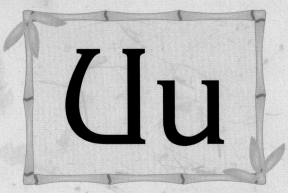

Uu

U is for umbrellas.

Umbrellas in China are for keeping both rain *and* sun off people's heads. Chinese people have been using them for more than 1,300 years. China's first umbrellas were made of bamboo and oiled paper. Artisans carefully painted them with beautiful, bright designs.

V v

V is for villages.

Most people in China live in villages. They work long hours all year long to grow food for the huge number of people who live in China. Much of the farming in China is still done by hand. In some areas, farmers use water buffalo to help plow the fields.

FAST FACT: People in villages are not as rich as people in the cities. In some villages, children have to share textbooks at school.

Ww

Early in the morning, thousands of Chinese people gather together at parks to practice wushu, or martial arts, together. Martial arts were invented hundreds of years ago as ways of fighting or defending oneself. Today people also practice wushu to exercise their bodies and relax their minds.

FAST FACT: *Each kind of Chinese martial arts has its own style. Some are like wrestling or boxing. Tai Chi (ty-jee) looks like a slow, graceful dance.*

26

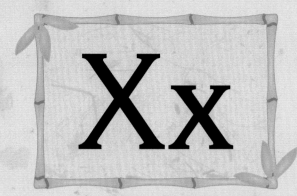

Xx

X is for *xiongmao* (shung–mau).

The Chinese call panda bears *xiongmao,* which means "bear cats." China's bamboo forests are the only place in the world where pandas can live in the wild. A panda bear needs to eat about 40 pounds (18 kilograms) of bamboo plants every day.

FAST FACT: *There are fewer than 1,000 pandas living in the wild. People all around the world are trying to save China's panda bears.*

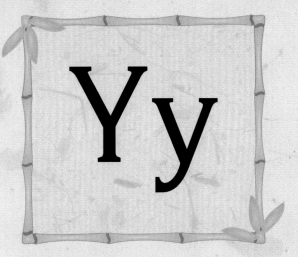

Yy

Y is for yuan (YOO–ahn).

The basic unit of Chinese money is the yuan. One yuan is made up of 10 jiao. Each jiao is made up of 10 fen. Chinese money comes in coins and bills.

FAST FACT: *Yuan bills are among the few kinds of money in the world with pictures of women on them.*

Z is for zodiac.

The Chinese zodiac is an ancient way of keeping track of years. Each year within a 12-year period is given the name of an animal. For example, 2004 is called the Year of the Monkey, and 2003 was the Year of the Sheep. In China, a polite way of finding out someone's age is to ask them the name of the year in which they were born.

rat 1924 1936 1948 1960 1972 1984 1996 2008	**ox** 1925 1937 1949 1961 1973 1985 1997 2009	**tiger** 1926 1938 1950 1962 1974 1986 1998 2010	**rabbit** 1927 1939 1951 1963 1975 1987 1999 2011
dragon 1928 1940 1952 1964 1976 1988 2000 2012	**snake** 1929 1941 1953 1965 1977 1989 2001 2013	**horse** 1930 1942 1954 1966 1978 1990 2002 2014	**sheep** 1931 1943 1955 1967 1979 1991 2003 2015
monkey 1932 1944 1956 1968 1980 1992 2004 2016	**rooster** 1933 1945 1957 1969 1981 1993 2005 2017	**dog** 1934 1946 1958 1970 1982 1994 2006 2018	**boar** 1935 1947 1959 1971 1983 1995 2007 2019

Can you find the animal of your birth year? In China, some people believe that animal tells something about your personality. Your animal is your "sign," just as Capricorn, Leo, or Virgo might be someone's sign in North America.

China in Brief

Official name: People's Republic of China

Capital: Beijing (13.8 million people)

Official language: Mandarin Chinese

Population: 1.25 billion

People: Han Chinese make up 93% of the population; 55 ethnic minorities make up the rest.

Main religions: Buddhism, Confucianism, Taoism

Education: Children must go to school for at least nine years, starting at age 6 or 7.

Major holidays: Chinese New Year and Lantern Festival (late January or early February); Tomb Sweeping Day (April); Dragon Boat Festival (June or July); Mid-Autumn Festival (October)

Transportation: Most people travel on bicycles, motorcycles, city buses, or trains.

Climate: The weather ranges from very hot to very cold, depending on location and season.

Area: 3,705,386 square miles (9,596,906 square kilometers)—a little big bigger than the United States

Highest point: Mount Everest, 29,035 feet (8,850 meters)

Lowest point: Turpan Depression, 505 feet (154 meters) below sea level

Type of government: communist republic

Head of government: Communist Party leader

Major industries: coal mining, food processing, machinery, textiles

Natural resources: coal, iron ore, petroleum

Major agricultural products: rice, wheat, potatoes, tea, cotton, pork

Chief exports: clothing, shoes, toys, electronics

National flower: peony

Money: yuan

Say It in Mandarin Chinese

bad . . . .*boo-how*

cat . . . . *mao* (rhymes with wow)

dog . . . .*go*

good luck! . . . . *jew-nee-how-yun*

good morning . . . . *zow-chen-how*

good night . . . . *wahn-ahn*

great! . . . . *tie-how*

tea . . . .*cha*

thank you . . . .*shee-shee*

Glossary

Buddhism—a religion that follows the teachings of an ancient spiritual teacher named Buddha. Buddhism started about 2,500 years ago.

characters—symbols used for writing Chinese words

communism—a way of running a country in which the government owns almost everything

dynasty—a period of time during which a country's rulers all come from one family

emperor—a kind of ruler who is like a king

martial arts—ancient Chinese methods for fighting or defending oneself

To Learn More

At the Library

Compestine, Ying Chang. *The Story of Chopsticks*. New York: Holiday House, 2001.

Salas, Laura Purdie. *China*. Mankato, Minn.: Bridgestone Books, 2002.

Simonds, Nina. *Moonbeams, Dumplings & Dragon Boats: A Treasury of Chinese Holiday Tales, Activities & Recipes*. San Diego: Harcourt, Inc., 2002.

Sis, Peter. *Tibet: Through the Red Box*. New York: Farrar Straus Giroux, 1998.

Tsubakiyama, Margaret. *Mei-Mei Loves the Morning*. Morton Grove, Ill.: Albert Whitman, 1999.

On the Web

FactHound offers a safe, fun way to find Web sites related to topics in this book. All of the sites on FactHound have been researched by our staff.

1. Visit *www.facthound.com*
2. Enter in this special code: 1404801804
3. Click on the FETCH IT button.

Your trusty FactHound will fetch the best sites for you!

Index